DEPARTMENT OF THE NAVY
HEADQUARTERS UNITED STATES MARINE CORPS
3000 MARINE CORPS PENTAGON
WASHINGTON, DC 20350-3000

I0440897

MARINE CORPS DIRECTIVES MANAGEMENT PROGRAM

DEPARTMENT OF THE NAVY
HEADQUARTERS UNITED STATES MARINE CORPS
3000 MARINE CORPS PENTAGON
WASHINGTON, DC 20350-3000

MCO 5215.1K
ARDB
10 MAY 2007

MARINE CORPS ORDER 5215.1K

From: Commandant of the Marine Corps
To: Distribution List

Subj: MARINE CORPS DIRECTIVES MANAGEMENT PROGRAM

Ref: (a) DOD Directive 5025.1, "DOD Directives System," July 14, 2004
       (b) SECNAVINST 5215.1D
       (c) MCWP 5-1, Appendix G
       (d) SECNAV M-5210.1
       (e) MCO P1070.12K
       (f) SECNAVINST 5216.5D
       (g) DOD 5025.1-M, Appendix 1, "DOD Directives System Procedures," March 5, 2003
       (h) U.S. Government Printing Office (GPO) Style Manual (2000), 29th Edition
       (i) JCS Publication 1-02, "DOD Dictionary of Military and Associated Terms," April 12, 2001
       (j) SECNAV M-5210.2
       (k) SECNAV M-5510.36
       (l) MCO 5214.2E
       (m) MCO P5600.31G
       (n) MCO 5213.7C
       (o) MCO 5213.8
       (p) SECNAVINST 5720.42F
       (q) OPNAVINST 5215.17

Encl: (1) Marine Corps Directives Management Program Procedural Guidance

1. Situation. To provide policy and procedural guidance for issuance of Marine Corps directives, per references (a) through (p). Orders and Bulletins hereafter are referred to collectively as "directives." Marine Corps sponsors of directives issued by the Secretary of the Navy shall refer to reference (q) for policy and procedural guidance.

2. Cancellation. MCO 5215.1J.

3. Mission. This Order provides policy for the preparation, approval, and maintenance of Marine Corps directives. All Marine Corps directives shall be written in compliance with this Order. Policy and procedural or "how to" guidance is contained in enclosure (1).

4. Execution

    a. Commander's Intent and Concept of Operations

        (1) Commander's Intent

             (a) The Marine Corps shall maintain a single, streamlined,

uniform system for the preparation, approval, and maintenance of directives. Detailed definitions, policy, and procedures are contained in the enclosure.

(b) <u>Designation of Directives</u>

<u>1</u>. All Headquarters Marine Corps (HQMC) directives shall be issued in the name of the Commandant of the Marine Corps. Marine Corps directives shall be issued as an "Order" or "Bulletin". HQMC directives shall be issued using the designation "Marine Corps Order" (MCO) or "Marine Corps Bulletin" (MCBul), as appropriate.

<u>2</u>. Field commands shall issue local directives in the name of the Commander using the designation line of the command issuing the directive; e.g., I Marine Expeditionary Force (MEF) Order (IMEFO) or I Marine Expeditionary Force (MEF) Bulletin (IMEFBul).

(2) <u>Concept of Operations</u>

(a) Current directives will not be revised for the sole purpose of complying with this Order.

(b) As directives are revised they shall comply with this Order.

(c) A directive shall not have more than 9 changes. A change can and should be issued when less than 50 percent of the total number of pages is modified. The directive shall be revised when a directive exceeds 9 changes, or if 50 percent or more of the total number of pages are modified.

(d) Issue changes (e.g., MCO 5215.1J Ch 1, MCO 5215.1J Ch 2) to directives published prior to this Order in the same format that it was issued.

(e) Sponsors will ensure directives under their purview comply with this Order.

(f) <u>Internal Reviews</u>. Sponsors shall review their directives annually to ensure they are necessary, current, and consistent with statutory authority. The results of the review shall be documented per the enclosure and retained according to reference (d).

(g) <u>Mandatory Coordination at HQMC</u>

<u>1</u>. All directives signed by CMC, ACMC, or DMCS shall be reviewed by the Counsel for the Commandant prior to signature.

<u>2</u>. All HQMC directives, changes, and revisions shall be fully coordinated with the appropriate HQMC staff agencies/offices and, when applicable, Marine Corps field commands and other external government agencies that the sponsor deems necessary. When directives require signature by the CMC or ACMC, the DMCS will determine any additional coordination that may be required.

<u>3</u>. Upon completion of initial staffing and resolution of comments, the sponsor shall send the original unsigned copy of the directive, the verbatim digitized version of the directive, and all background material for signature. If any changes are required, the complete package will

be sent back to the sponsor for correction. Upon signature, the final package will be sent to CMC (ARDB) for publishing.

    b. <u>Subordinate Element Missions</u>

       (1) <u>CMC (ARDB) shall</u>:

         (a) Make policy, manage, and administer the Marine Corps Directives Management Program, to include issuing procedures for preparing, staffing, approving, and maintaining Marine Corps Directives.

         (b) Issue standard formats for Marine Corps directives.

         (c) Review all HQMC directives prior to signature for format and compliance with the policy and procedural guidance in this Order. Upon completion, provide the directive's sponsor with a signed NAVMC HQ 942 (Rev. 12/06), Clearance of Proposed Issuance (CPI) that either approves, approves subject to mark-up/comments, or disapproves the directive for publishing. NAVMC HQ 942 may be obtained on the Marine Corps Electronic Forms web site at http://www.hqmc.usmc.mil/ar/mcefs.nsf.

         (d) Maintain, preserve, and retire the signed original copy of all HQMC directives, all background materials, and all staffing comments per reference (d).

         (e) Conduct a triennial review of HQMC Marine Corps Orders (MCOs) to determine whether to update, revise, consolidate, or cancel, as appropriate.

       (2) <u>Sponsors of HQMC directives and field commanders shall</u>:

         (a) Comply with this Order when preparing, reviewing, staffing, and promulgating directives.

         (b) Enter distribution data for issuances into the Marine Corps Publications Distribution System.

         (c) Ensure that directives requiring records disposition instructions, reports, and use of forms/formats are cleared by the HQMC program manager or command's staff designated to perform such duties.

         (d) Conduct a Directives Review

           <u>1</u>. Review directives to revise, combine similar subjects into one directive, issue a change, or cancel as appropriate.

           <u>2</u>. Revise an order when it is 9 years old; do not republish just for that reason.

           <u>3</u>. Review and update a directive when it previously supplemented/implemented a higher authority's directive that has been modified.

           <u>4</u>. Justify and document your records when a directive cannot be updated or cancelled; monitor target dates for completion or cancellation.

     5. Review directives on their anniversary dates or at a set time each year. When a new change is issued, review the basic directive and any changes.

     6. Stock directives in adequate supply for requests from internal staff offices, subordinate units, and field commands or installations.

     7. Activities issuing directives shall use the NAVMC 10974, Directives Review form, or an automated tracking system to document the annual review of local directives. See enclosure (1), chapter (1), paragraph 14c.

     8. When a bulletin has a "Cancellation Contingency" paragraph (Chapter 3, paragraph 10g), prepare a NAVMC 10974. Attach the bulletin card to the current order card until the bulletin is incorporated in the order.

     9. Establish a Directives Control Point (DCP) to manage and administer the command directives management program. CMC (ARDB) will serve as the DCP for Headquarters directives. Field commands are required to designate a DCP in writing.

     10. Submit to the DCP the signed original copy of the directive, all background materials, and all staffing comments for retention per reference (d).

   (3) CMC (IG). Review implementation of the Marine Corps Directives Management Program during command inspections.

5. Administration and Logistics. Recommendations concerning the contents of this Order may be forwarded to CMC (ARDB) via the appropriate chain-of-command.

6. Command and Signal

  a. Command. This Order is applicable to the Marine Corps Total Force.

  b. Signal. This Order is effective the date signed.

R. S. KRAMLICH
Director, Marine Corps Staff

DISTRIBUTION: PCN 10207570000

  Copy to: 7000260 (2)
          7000144/8145001 (1)

LOCATOR SHEET

Subj: MARINE CORPS DIRECTIVES MANAGEMENT PROGRAM PROCEDURAL MANUAL

Location: _____
(Indicate the location(s) of the copy(ies) of this Order.)

RECORD OF CHANGES

Log completed change action as indicated.

Change Number	Date of Change	Date Entered	Signature of Person Incorporated Change

TABLE OF CONTENTS

TABLE OF CONTENTS

TABLE OF CONTENTS

Enclosure (1)

Chapter 1

Directives Administrative Procedures

1. <u>General</u>. This chapter provides detailed information on the policy, definitions, authorities, responsibilities, and procedures associated with the preparation of Marine Corps directives.

2. <u>Background</u>. The Marine Corps Directives Management Program shall be administered in accordance with this Order. Chapters 2 through 4 provide instructions and formats for preparing directives and other issuances.

3. <u>Definitions</u>

   a. <u>Directive</u>. A written communication for issuing policy and procedures.

   b. <u>Order</u>. An order is a directive of continuing authority or information, meant to be a permanent reference, and requiring continuing action. An order is directed to the command's overall functions rather than to individualized office functions. An Order shall:

      (1) Establish, describe, or change existing policy, programs and major activities, and organizations.

      (2) Define missions.

      (3) Delegate authority.

      (4) Assign responsibilities.

      (5) Issue procedural guidance, when necessary.

      (6) Be written in the 5-paragraph format as prescribed in reference (c) and this Order.

   c. <u>Bulletin</u>. A bulletin is a directive of a one-time or brief term, has the same force and effect as an order, may require a one-time report, and must have a self-canceling provision. It normally remains in effect up to 12 months, <u>but no longer</u>. Action required by a bulletin; e.g., submission of reports, use of forms, maintaining and disposing of records, or following a specific procedure, is cancelled when the bulletin cancels, unless the requirement is incorporated in another directive. If a bulletin with a given cancellation date has cancelled and the material is still required, reissue the material in another directive. Bulletins shall be written in the format prescribed in Chapter 3 of this Order.

   d. <u>Directives Issued in Message Format</u>. A bulletin or an advance change to an order that is of an urgent nature and may be transmitted via the Defense Messaging System and addressed to selected addressees, a Collective Address Designator (e.g, 'MARADMIN') or an Address List (AL).

   e. <u>Principal Official</u>. The senior official whose title appears in the "From:" line of a directive.

   f. <u>Assistant Principal</u>. An official who performs the duties of the principal during the latter's absence or disability, and performs such other duties as the principal directs.

g. <u>Executive Officer</u>. A senior official who directs, coordinates, and supervises the activities of HQMC or a command element and performs such duties as directed by the principal. Also, the executive officer performs the duties of the assistant principal in the latter's absence.

h. <u>Principal Subordinate</u>. An oversight authority who is responsible for implementing policy and programs as delegated by the principal official.

4. <u>Exemptions</u>. The documents below are not issued under the Marine Corps Directives Management Program.

a. Marine Corps Manual.

b. Technical publications, users' manuals, and NAVMC publications.

c. Stocklist publications.

d. Landing force, tactical, warfighting, and doctrinal publications.

e. Tables of organization and tables of equipment.

f. Combat plans, orders, and documents governing tactical operations.

g. Top secret material.

h. Special orders, travel orders, and courts-martial orders, etc.

i. Letters of instruction and programs of instruction.

j. CMC policy memorandums.

k. Requests for comments, approval, or information.

l. Material requiring special handling.

m. Material concerning non-Marine Corps commands.

n. Urgent communications concerning safety, security, or protection of individuals and/or equipment.

o. Public affairs events.

p. General announcements and information.

q. Output of data systems material which is needed for the proper operation of computer systems.

5. <u>Promulgation of Supplemental Directives</u>

a. Supplemental directives shall not contradict, repeat (unless required by the higher authority's directive), or enclose the higher authority's directive.

b. Do not issue supplements when the higher authority's directive provides complete details; however, clarification and implementation guidance may be issued as needed. The supplemental directive must incorporate by reference the higher authority's directive.

c. Do not issue supplements below the battalion or squadron level on the following subjects (exception: separately detached commands or Inspectors-Instructors may issue supplements as needed to satisfy unit mission or geographical requirements):

(1) Leave and Liberty.

(2) Assumption of Command.

(3) Alcoholic beverage control.

(4) Mail Handling instructions (applicable only to commands operating unit mailrooms).

(5) Command security procedures, per reference (k) (not applicable if your command is not authorized or does not have the capability to secure classified material).

6. Authority to Issue Directives. All commanders, per the Marine Corps Manual, including officers in charge, are authorized to issue directives in their own directives system within their immediate organization or command as needed for efficient operation, except where responsibility is retained by higher authority. Directives will be issued under the title of the principal official of the organization or command. HQMC activities and field commands must refer to figure 2-2 for formatting.

7. Delegating Signature Authority. The principal official may delegate signature authority "by title" to senior officials, to military and civilian subordinates, and may authorize those subordinates to delegate signature authority further. When signature authority is delegated further, those officials will sign "By direction." Delegating signature authority must be in writing, to titles rather than names. See Chapter 4 for signature authority for joint directives.

a. HQMC. HQMC directives will be signed by the principal official (CMC), the assistant principal (ACMC), or the executive officer (Director, Marine Corps Staff (DMCS)). The HQMC principal subordinates listed below (or the person 'Acting' for that official) are authorized to sign HQMC directives for matters solely within their departmental area of responsibility and which good judgment indicates need not be forwarded to higher authority. Signature authority may not be redelegated.

(1) "By title:"

Deputy Commandant for Aviation
Deputy Commandant for Manpower and Reserve Affairs
Deputy Commandant for Combat Development and Integration
Deputy Commandant for Programs and Resources
Deputy Commandant for Plans, Policies and Operations
Deputy Commandant for Installations and Logistics
Counsel for the Commandant

Director, Command, Control, Communications and Computers
Director, Intelligence
Director, Public Affairs
Staff Judge Advocate to the Commandant
Legislative Assistant to the Commandant
Inspector General of the Marine Corps

(2) "By direction:"

Commanding General, Marine Corps Combat Development Command
Commanding General, Marine Corps Recruiting Command
Commanding General, Marine Corps Systems Command
Commanding General, Training and Education Command
Assistant Deputy Commandant for Aviation
Assistant Deputy Commandant for Manpower and Reserve Affairs
Assistant Deputy Commandant for Combat Development and
   Integration
Assistant Deputy Commandant for Programs and Resources
   (Fiscal Director)
Assistant Deputy Commandant for Plans, Policies and Operations
Assistant Deputy Commandant for Installations and Logistics
Director, Personnel Management Division (MM)
Director, Manpower Plans and Policy Division (MP)
Director, Reserve Affairs Division (RA)
Director, Manpower Management Information Systems Division (MI)
Director, Personal and Family Readiness Division (MR)
President, Marine Corps Permanent Uniform Board
Director, Administration and Resource Management Division
Director, Marine Corps History and Museums Division

   b. Field Commands. Field command directives shall be approved and signed by the principal official or delegate. Refer to page 1-3, paragraph 7 of this Order for delegation of signature authority.

8. Directives Control Point (DCP). HQMC staff agencies and field commanders shall establish a DCP to comply with the responsibilities and procedures detailed for processing directives. Field commands are required to designate a DCP in writing. CMC (ARDB) is the DCP for HQMC directives.

9. Classified Directives

   a. A classified directive shall be formatted in the same manner as an unclassified directive with the following inclusion. Refer to reference (k) for classification markings.

   b. An abbreviated security classification of the directive shall precede the Standard Subject Identification code (SSIC) ("C" for confidential and "S" for secret; e.g., MCO C5215.1, MCO S5215.1).

   c. Sponsor must load distribution list to Marine Corps Publications and Distribution System (MCPDS) as these will remain hard copy and contain the appropriate Distribution Statement on the first page.

10. Designation "FOR OFFICIAL USE ONLY" (FOUO) Directives

     a. The abbreviation "FOUO" shall be used to designate unclassified portions containing information exempt from mandatory release to the public under references (k) and (p).

     b. Center and type in all capital letters "FOR OFFICIAL USE ONLY" at the bottom of the letterhead page and the last printed page on a directive when all information is FOUO.

     c. Show the FOUO designation on front and back covers of binders, and the reverse side of the last page.

     d. Start the FOUO two lines below the page number, but do not exceed the typing area of the page.

     e. When a portion of the directive is FOUO, show the designation on all affected pages. Additionally, follow the examples below for proper citing at bottom of the letterhead page and center:

FOR OFFICIAL USE ONLY
Designation is cancelled upon removal of pages 10-11 to 10-20
and 11-3 to 11-10.
OR
FOR OFFICIAL USE ONLY
Designation is cancelled upon removal of chapters 3 and 6.

OR
FOR OFFICIAL USE ONLY
Designation is cancelled upon removal of pages 3 and 4 of the
basic directive and enclosures (1) and (4).

---

11. Directive Sponsor Change

     a. Report a change in sponsor of a directive via email to the DCP when the change is within the same organization.

     b. If the change is to a different organization, send the email to the DCP via the new sponsor for formal concurrence.

12. Command Relocation or Re-designation. Do not republish existing directives just to change the address or title of a command.

13. Command Assumption. An assumption of command directive may be in letter or order format. When issued as an order, follow the example in chapter 1, figure 1-1. A command directives review shall be conducted up to 1 year after the principal officer has assumed command.

14. Internal Reviews

     a. Directives shall be reviewed annually to ensure that they are necessary; current; and consistent with Marine Corps policy, existing law, and statutory authority.

b. Upon completion of the review, the sponsors shall certify whether the directives shall be continued, revised, or cancelled.

c. Record the results of the review of your directives on NAVMC 10974 (Rev. 11/06), Directives Review card, including those that supplement a higher authority directive. NAVMC 10974 may be obtained on the Marine Corps Electronic Forms web site at http://www.hqmc.usmc.mil/ar/mcefs.nsf. Use the card until the last edition is canceled. Pencil in a new revision letter or change number and the new date. When the order cancels, move the card to a canceled file; check this file to avoid reassigning the consecutive point number. Commands may use an automated database file containing the same information as an option to recording the results of the review on a NAVMC 10974.

15. Gender Specific Language and Personal Pronouns

a. Use the phrase "he and she," rather than writing "he" or "she" separately as generic pronouns.

b. Do not use the personal pronouns "I" and "me."

c. Use "Marine," "member," "student," "spouse," "officer," "personnel," "applicant," etc., when the directive is applicable to both male and female.

d. Indicate the gender in the subject line, purpose paragraph, or enclosure title, etc., when the directive or that portion pertains to a specific gender.

16. Abbreviations, Acronyms, and Reference Aids

a. Type out the full name of any acronyms or abbreviations used and place the acronym or abbreviation in parentheses the first time it appears in the text. The first use of abbreviations and acronyms in any chapter applies to all subsequent chapters.

b. Do not use an acronym if it is not repeated.

c. In military abbreviations/acronyms, use commas only before the city and state; e.g., CG MCLB, Albany, GA. Omit the comma with the shortened name of a military command; e.g., CG MCCDC, CG MARCORSYSCOM, M&RA (MMPR).

d. Directives should contain a glossary of acronyms and abbreviations, when numerous, in an appendix.

e. Use the following resources when you have questions about punctuation, capitalization, spelling, numerals, compound words, use of military terms, acronyms, etc.: (Note: The words "order" and "bulletin" are only capitalized in the text when it is referring to itself.)

(1) U.S. Government Printing Office Style Manual (GPO Style Manual) http://www.gpoaccess.gov/stylemanual/browse.html. This manual contains the preferred spelling of certain words, rules for punctuation, compounding, citing numerals, capitalization, plurals of acronyms, etc.

(2) Word Division Supplement to the GPO Style Manual. This supplement contains basic rules for dividing words at the ends of lines and has a quick reference aid list for dividing words into syllables.

(3) JCS Pub 1-02, Department of Defense Dictionary of Military and Associated Terms http://www.dtic.mil/doctrine/jel/new_pubs/jp1_02.pdf. This publication contains the authority for the definition and usage of military terms.

(4) MCO P1070.12K, Individual Records Administration Manual (IRAM) This Manual contains a list of acronyms and abbreviations that apply to the Marine Corps. If an abbreviation is not listed in the IRAM, use JCS Pub 1-02 or GPO Style Manual. Do not use acronyms/abbreviations for any words not in the directives or manuals in this paragraph or not commonly used Marine Corps-wide.

17. Staffing and Clearing Directives

    a. HQMC directives sponsors and all command levels are responsible for ensuring all comments, recommendations, concurrences, and non-concurrences have been incorporated or resolved, and that their directives are modified, when required.

    b. Send the directive to the DCP for format and editorial review and approval to forward for signature when it has been approved at each review level of the sponsor's chain-of-command and finalized for signature. Once signed, the sponsor must insert the date signed (day-month-year) under the sponsor code on the cover letter of the directive identification in the upper right corner. A date stamp may be used to insert the date on the cover page. The same format must be used on all subsequent pages of the directive leaving out the sponsor code.

    c. For classified directives or those that cannot be published electronically, type the directive identification in the upper right corner of odd numbered pages and upper left corner of even numbered pages. Otherwise, directive identification is to be placed in the upper right corner of all pages.

    d. Forward the verbatim digitized version of the directive with the original, all background material, and comments/recommendations to the appropriate DCP to process for distribution and/or publishing.

18. Letterhead Stationery and Style of Type

    a. Stationery for Directives

        (1) HQMC Staff Agencies

            (a) Print the first page of Marine Corps directives emanating from the Commandant of the Marine Corps on the official Marine Corps letterhead stationery, i.e., DEPARTMENT OF THE NAVY, HEADQUARTERS UNITED STATES MARINE CORPS, 3000 MARINE CORPS PENTAGON, WASHINGTON, DC 20350-3000.

            (b) Use letter-size plain bond paper for all additional pages.

(2) Field Commands

(a) Use the official command or unit letterhead stationery for the first page. If none is available, type the unit's letterhead in all upper case letters beginning 5/8 of an inch from the top edge of the paper and center all lines.

(b) Use letter-size plain bond paper for all additional pages.

b. Size and Style of Type. Use Courier or Courier New typeface; 10 or 12 point.

c. Margins. Margins are the same as for a naval letter, i.e., top, bottom, left, right, and header must be 1 inch and bottom footer must be 1/2 inch. Page numbers must be centered in bottom footer. When a directive has enclosure(s) or attachment(s) that are in "landscape", the margins vary for text, table diagram, etc., to fit properly.

d. Electronic Letterhead. Refer to reference (f) CH-2, Appendix C.

19. Distribution Statements. Directives sponsors shall designate distribution of their directives using one of the distribution statements:

DISTRIBUTION STATEMENT A: Approved for public release; distribution is unlimited.

DISTRIBUTION STATEMENT B: Distribution authorized to U.S. Government agencies only; (fill in reason) (date of determination). Other requests for this document will be referred to (insert originating command).

DISTRIBUTION STATEMENT C: Distribution authorized to U.S. Government agencies and their contractors; (fill in reason) (date of determination). Other requests for this document will be referred to (insert originating command).

DISTRIBUTION STATEMENT D: Distribution authorized to DOD and DOD contractors only; (fill in reason) (date of determination). Other U.S. requests shall be referred to (insert originating command).

DISTRIBUTION STATEMENT E: Distribution authorized to DOD components only; (fill in reason) (date of determination). Other requests must be referred to (insert originating command).

DISTRIBUTION STATEMENT F: Further dissemination only as directed by (insert originating command) (date of determination) or higher DOD authority.

DISTRIBUTION STATEMENT X: Distribution authorized to U.S. Government agencies and private individuals or enterprises eligible to obtain export-controlled technical data in accordance with OPNAVINST 5510.161; (date of determination). Other requests shall be referred to (originating command).

---

20. Printing and Distribution

a. Distribution "A" directives are no longer printed for mass distribution. Unclassified directives that are unlimited release, Distribution Statement "A" are posted on the Marine Corps Publications Electronic Library (MCPEL) Web site and CD-ROM. Unclassified directives that are other than Distribution Statement "A" are printed for distribution.

b. For Official Use Only (FOUO) and classified directives are published in paper format. The originating office determines the distribution of these documents (see paragraph above). These directives shall not be placed on an unclassified web site.

21. Preparing Directives. Prepare directives per the following administrative instructions:

a. Directive Identification Block. On the cover page, place the abbreviated directive type (e.g., MCO XXXX, 2DMARDIVO), SSIC, point number, and revision, if applicable, in the upper right corner beginning on the line below the last line of the letterhead. Type command or sponsor code on the next line. Insert the date signed under the command or sponsor after the directive is signed. Show the date in day-month-year format, using the first three letters of the month and two or four digits of the year; e.g., 31 Aug 2003 or 31 Aug 03. A date stamp may be used to insert the date on the cover page.

b. Numbering System. Use reference (j) to select the proper directive number. The directive sponsor selects the SSIC; however, the DCP verifies that the SSIC is appropriate or not already in use.

c. Numbering Composition. The numbering system is composed of the SSIC, four or five-digit number representing a major subject group and its subgroup, followed by a consecutive point and the sequential number of the subgroup; e.g., for MCO 5215.1K, the directive is the major subject group "5200," the number "15" represents the subgroup, and the number "1" indicates that the directive is the first directive assigned to that subgroup.

d. Consecutive Point Number

(1) The DCP assigns a new consecutive point number after directives have been signed. The consecutive point number indicates only the sequence of issue within each SSIC; it has no relation to the subject of the directive. Consecutive point numbers of cancelled directives are not reissued.

(2) The consecutive point number may be assigned before a directive is signed. Record the number to avoid duplicating numbers.

(3) Upon revision of P-type HQMC MCOs the "P" will be removed; e.g., MCO PXXXX.XX will become MCO XXXX.XX.

(4) Because bulletins are effective for 12 or fewer months, they are not assigned a consecutive point number. Bulletins are identified by their SSIC and the date issued; e.g., MCBul 5215 of 24 Nov 2006. Directives issuing activities shall not issue more than one bulletin per day with the same SSIC.

e. Revisions

(1) Identify revisions of directives by a capital letter; e.g., the first revision MCO 5215.1A, the second MCO 5215.1B, etc. Do not use the letters "I", "O", and "Q" as suffixes to revisions.

(2) Use the lowest consecutive point number for a revision when it cancels two or more directives bearing the same SSIC; e.g., MCO 5215.15A is assigned when it cancels MCO 5215.15, MCO 5215.16, and MCO 5215.25.

(3) Use the lowest consecutive number of a revision when it cancels two or more directives bearing <u>different</u> SSICs; e.g., MCO 5200.5B is assigned when it cancels MCO 5200.5A, MCO 5200.10, MCO 5230.9, and MCO 5233.7.

(4) When a directive is an edition "Z" and is revised, assign the next available "basic" consecutive point number (without an alpha suffix) within the same SSIC; e.g., MCO 5215.5Z is revised to MCO 5215.6, if .6 has not been assigned to another directive. If .6 has been assigned to another directive, then use the next available unassigned point number.

22. <u>Reserve Designation</u>. Include an "R" after the SSIC when a directive applies only to the Marine Corps Reserve; e.g., MCO 5215R.15.

23. <u>Designation Line</u>. Start the designation line on the second line below the date in all capital letters, and underlined as shown below:

<u>MARINE CORPS ORDER 5215.1K</u>

---

a. "<u>From:</u>" Line. Use the title of the principal official.

b. "<u>To:</u>" Line. Insert "Distribution List."

c. "<u>Subj:</u>" Line. When typing the "Subj:" line do the following:

(1) Type subject line in all capital letters.

(2) Give a topical statement that best reflects the contents or purpose.

(3) Write out the full name of any acronyms or abbreviations used, and place the acronym or abbreviation in parentheses.

**<u>MARINE CORPS ORDER 5215.1K</u> or
<u>MARINE CORPS BULLETIN 5215</u>**

**From: Commandant of the Marine Corps
To: Distribution List**

Subj: MARINE CORPS DIRECTIVES MANAGEMENT PROGRAM (MCDMP)

---

24. "<u>Ref:</u>" Section

a. Start the "Ref:" section on the second line below the last line of the subject.

b. List references in the same sequence in which they first appear in the text of the basic directive. All references must be used in the text.

c. List references by directive type, SSIC or document number, and title/subject. Title/subject may be either enclosed in parentheses or preceded by a comma in a uniform manner followed by the effective date of the directive. List the directive type and SSIC or document number only, for Navy and Marine Corps directives. Samples of format and style of reference citations of DOD directives are listed in reference (g).

d. Cite only current references and show the alpha suffix of the edition (do not list unpublished material, such as drafts and documents that are not usually available to readers). A reference must be signed/dated before or on the same day as the proposed directive.

e. When citing bulletins, MARADMINs, or any correspondence with an expiration date as a reference in a directive, place the cancellation date in parenthesis; i.e., (canc: Aug 06).

f. When a directive contains more than 26 references, use a double lettering system; e.g., (aa)-(az).

25. <u>Citing References</u>. Use the term "reference (a)" or "references (b) and (c)." (See reference (f).)

26. "Encl:" Section

a. Start the "Encl:" section on the second line below the last line of the "Ref:" section.

b. The enclosure title in this section must read exactly the same as shown on the actual enclosure.

c. Use initial capital letters for main words, but do not capitalize articles, conjunctions, or two and three-letter prepositions.

d. List enclosures in the same sequence in which they first appear in the text of the basic directive.

27. <u>Citing Enclosures</u>

a. <u>Letterhead Through Signature Pages of a Directive</u>. Use the term "enclosure (1)" or "enclosures (1) and (2)." (See reference (f)).

b. Type the SSIC, date, enclosure identification, and page number on the front page of a preprinted document of a different agency when it is to be printed with the directive.

28. <u>Locator Sheet</u>. (Optional for unclassified directives.)

a. The locator sheet is the next page after the promulgation page of the directive; e.g., "i".

b. File this sheet like a directive in the master directives file to indicate the physical location of the directive when it is filed external of the master directives file.

c. Prepare a locator sheet for classified directives or when deemed necessary.

d. Do not use locator sheets in place of "charge out" cards.

e. If a joint military service directive does not have a locator sheet and will be filed elsewhere, prepare two, if needed; file one in the master directives file, the other in the applicable military services directives file.

29. "Report(s) Required:" Section

a. Any communication that imposes reporting requirements (regardless of form) on addressees will be promulgated under the Marine Corps Directives Management Program. See reference (l) for additional information.

b. Orders and Bulletins

(1) Start the "Report(s) Required:" section before the first paragraph.

(2) Type the report title, report control symbol (in parentheses), and paragraph or show the enclosure number (no more than four reports on the promulgation page), particularly when orders covering the report are not shown on the letterhead page.

> **Report(s) Required:**   **Review of Publications (Report Control Symbol MC-5215-01), par. 2a**
> **OR**
> **Reports Required:**   **I. Periodic Review of Approved Reports (Report Control Symbol DN-5214-02), par. 4b**

(3) When there are five or more reports, list them in an enclosure in the same sequence in which they first appear in the text of the basic directive.

> **Reports Required:**   **See enclosure (2)**
> **(When there are more than four reports.)**

(4) Type the report control symbol in an appropriate position on forms used for submission of reports. Use a "Report(s) Required:" section for a report that is exempted.

(5) Do not show the report control symbol in the text when the directive is only one page.

c. When there are up to four reports, follow the report format in paragraph 29b(2), above. When there are more than four reports, list them on a separate page as shown on the next page:

```
+-----------------------------------------------------------------------+
|                          Reports Required                             |
|                                                                       |
|                           REPORT                                      |
|   REPORT TITLE            CONTROL SYMBOL           PARAGRAPH           |
|                                                                       |
|    I.  Xxxxx Xxx Xxxxxx   MC-5215-01               2                   |
|                                                                       |
|   II.  Xxxxxx Xxxxxxx Xxx MC-5215-02               3a                  |
|                                                                       |
|  III.  Xxx Xxxx Xxxxxxx   EXEMPT                   4b(2)(a)            |
|                                                                       |
|   IV.  Xx Xxxx Xxxxx      MC 5215-03               encl. (1)          |
|                                                                       |
|    V.  Xxx Xxxx Xxxxx     MC-5215-04               encl. (2)          |
|                                                                       |
+-----------------------------------------------------------------------+
```

Show the report(s) required section on the promulgation page as follows:

```
+------------------------------------+
| Reports Required:  List, page v.   |
+------------------------------------+
```

30. Forms Management

     a. Any communication that prescribes the use of an official blank form will be issued by a directive and cleared, before signature, through the responsible office assigned those duties. A "Forms" paragraph will be incorporated in the directive identifying the form type, number, title, source of supply, and stock number if applicable.

     b. Local reproduction is not authorized for official blank forms that are available from an official supply source. Forms that are not available or stocked are not authorized. Refer to references (n) and (o) for policy and procedural guidance.

     c. If a new form cannot be stocked in the official supply system in sufficient time to meet the users deadlines, the sponsor will make an initial distribution to the activities that need the form.

31. Records Disposition. Any communication that imposes a requirement to create and/or maintain records (regardless of form) will be issued by a directive and will include instructions to dispose of these records, per reference (d).

32. Paragraphs. Refer to chapters 2 through 3 for required paragraphs.

     a. Do not right justify margins.

     b. Use one or two-digit Arabic numerals for major paragraph numbers.

     c. Include a title for all major paragraphs.

     d. Show titles for subparagraphs, if needed.

     e. Underline all paragraph titles.

     f. Do not use punctuation after a paragraph title that stands alone.

g. Use initial capital letters for all key words of paragraph titles.

h. When a paragraph is subdivided, it must have at least two subdivisions; e.g., paragraph 1 must have subparagraphs 1a and 1b, etc.

i. Do not break the final word of any paragraph or at the end of a page. Do not leave a paragraph title and/or its subtitle at the end of a page, it must be followed by at least two consecutive lines of text.

33. <u>Paragraph Numbering System</u>. Arrange paragraphs following the format on the next page:

1.**Arrange paragraphs following the formats below.
%
2.**If subparagraphs are needed, use at least two; e.g., a(1) must have a
(2).
%
****a.**Indent each subdivision four spaces and start typing at the fifth
space.
%
****b.**Text.
%
********(1)*Documents rarely require subdividing to the extent shown below.
%
********(2)*Text.
%
***********(a)*Do not subparagraph past this level unless you have exhausted
all reparagraphing.
%
***********(b)*Text.
%
***************<u>1</u>.**Text.
%
******************<u>a</u>.**Text.
%
**********************(<u>1</u>)*Text.
%
***************************(<u>a</u>)*Never subparagraph beyond this level.
%
***************************(<u>b</u>)*Text.
%
**********************(<u>2</u>)*Text.
%
******************<u>b</u>.**Text.
%
***************<u>2</u>.**Text.
%
10.**When using two digits, continue to indent each new subdivision four
spaces and start typing on the fifth space (paragraphs will not
line up).

NOTE:
* AN ASTERISK (*) INDICATES A SINGLE BLANK SPACE.
% A PERCENT SIGN (%) INDICATES A SINGLE BLANK LINE.

34. Optional Paragraph Numbering for Directives with Enclosures over 200 Pages: The following optional paragraph numbering is authorized for use within directives with enclosures larger than 200 pages: A major paragraph must be identified by either a four or five digit number. Put a period at the end of the paragraph number (i.e. 3018.) and allow two character spaces before typing the paragraph title. Begin the first major paragraph of the first chapter with the four-digit number "1000" (preferred) or "1001". Follow the diagram below when forming paragraphs:

```
                                                          3102.9c(3)(a)

Chapter ─────────────────────────────────────────────────┐   │ │ │ │
                                                              │ │ │ │
Section ──────────────────────────────────────────────────────┘ │ │ │
                                                                │ │ │
Paragraph─────────────────────────────────────────────────────────┘ │ │
                                                                    │ │
Subparagraph──────────────────────────────────────────────────────────┘
```

NOTE: The first digit identifies the chapter number, the second digit the section number, and the third and fourth digits the paragraph number. The numbers following the decimal identify the subparagraph number.

35. Citing Paragraph Numbers in Text. Directives must cite paragraph numbers without periods and spaces; e.g., 1a(2)(b).

36. Spacing. Show one space after parentheses and two spaces after periods in the text of directives.

37. Signature Block, Distribution, and Copy to Sections. Show the signature block on the last page before enclosures, appendices, etc. There must be at least two consecutive lines of text on the same page as the signature. The "DISTRIBUTION:" and "Copy to:" sections must be shown on the signature page, if applicable.

    a. Use the principal's or the delegated principal subordinate's preference to compose the name, typed in all capital letters, or as preferred by the signatory, on the fifth line below the text. Start each line of the signature block at the center of the page. Do not use the signer's grade or rank.

        (1) Do not show the title of the principal officer (the person whose title appears in the "From:" line of the directive).

        (2) Include the title of a principal subordinate authorized to sign by title as shown on the next page:

```
┌─────────────────────────────────────────────────────────────────────────┐
│                                 HQMC                                       │
│                                                                            │
│  R. MAGNUS                 R. S. KRAMLICH              I. M. SUBORDINATE    │
│  Assistant Commandant      Director, Marine Corps Staff  Deputy Commandant for │
│  of the Marine Corps                                  Aviation            │
│                                                                            │
│                            Field Commands                                  │
│                                                                            │
│  I. M. CHIEF               I. M. DEPUTY               I. M. EXECUTIVE      │
│  Chief of Staff            Deputy                     Executive Officer    │
│                                                                            │
└─────────────────────────────────────────────────────────────────────────┘
```

(3) Begin with the word "Acting" when the signer has been formally appointed or delegated to replace temporarily the principal or a principal subordinate who signs by title, as shown here:

```
┌─────────────────────────────────────────────────────────────────────────┐
│                                 HQMC                                       │
│                                                                            │
│  I. M. ACTING              I. M. ACTING                                     │
│  Acting                    Deputy Commandant for                          │
│                            Manpower and Reserve Affairs                    │
│                            Acting                                          │
│                                                                            │
│                            Field Commands                                  │
│                                                                            │
│  I. M. ACTING              I. M. ACTING               I. M. ACTING         │
│  Chief of Staff            Deputy                     Executive Officer    │
│  Acting                    Acting                     Acting              │
│                                                                            │
└─────────────────────────────────────────────────────────────────────────┘
```

   b. "DISTRIBUTION:" Section

      (1) Start on the second line below the last line of the signature block, in all capital letters, at the left margin.

      (2) Show your distribution and/or Individual Activity Codes (IACs) of units that must take action.

   c. "Copy to:" Section

      (1) Start on the second line below the last line of the distribution section, and line up the colon with the colon of the word "DISTRIBUTION:".

      (2) Show the IACs of units under your jurisdiction, as well as those that are not, as information addresses, if needed.

```
┌─────────────────────────────────────────────────────────────────────────┐
│                                                                            │
│   DISTRIBUTION:  PCN 10207570000                                           │
│                                                                            │
│        Copy to:  7000260 (2)                                               │
│                  8145001 (1)                                               │
│                                                                            │
└─────────────────────────────────────────────────────────────────────────┘
```

38. Identifying Additional Pages of the Basic Directive. For unclassified directives, type the directives identification block 1-inch from the top

right corner of each page as a header. For classified and printed
directives, the directive identification block alternates sides; upper left
on even numbered pages, and upper right on odd numbered pages. Alternating
sides for unclassified directives is optional. Show the directive date on
the next line, as shown below.

MCO 5215.1J	MCBul 5215
31 Aug 2003	2 Sep 2003

39. Numbering Pages. Center and number the second and succeeding pages
sequentially throughout the directive with an Arabic numeral 1/2 inch from
the bottom of the paper as a footer. Do not number the first page of
directives. Identify the first page of each enclosure in the bottom right
corner with the word "Enclosure (X)" and the appropriate enclosure number
inside the parenthesis.

40. Change Transmittals and Page Replacements

    a. Substantive Change. This type of change amends an essential portion
of a directive; such as, policy, applicability, responsibilities, purpose,
procedures, reports, and implementation. These changes must be coordinated
with organizations who have mutually-related responsibilities for
review and concurrence or comments.

    b. Administrative Change. Amends non-substantive portions of a
directive, such as date of references and organizational symbols. These
changes need not be coordinated.

41. Preparing a Change. Provide page replacements as follows:

    a. Prepare a change when less than 50 percent of the current pages are
modified. Issue a revision when changing more than 50 percent of the basic
directive.

    b. Promulgate a change to the respective directive when it amplifies,
cancels, or modifies its contents.

42. Change Transmittal Page. Follow the format of a directive, but
incorporate the following exceptions:

    a. Start the SSIC on the next line below the letterhead to include the
change number; e.g., MCO 5215.1J Ch 1. (See example in figure 1-2 of this
chapter.)

    b. Give each change a consecutive number; such as, Ch 1, Ch 2, etc.
Include the change number on the designation line as follows:

MARINE CORPS ORDER 5215.1J Ch 1

    c. "Encl:" Section. Use this section to transmit page replacements and
include the following:

```
┌─────────────────────────────────────────────────────────────────────┐
│   Encl:   (1) New page inserts to MCO 5215.1J                          │
│                                                                       │
└─────────────────────────────────────────────────────────────────────┘
```

d. "Situation" Paragraph. Tell what the change is doing; i.e., transmitting page inserts.

e. "Mission" Paragraph. Background and information paragraphs may be included when needed.

f. "Execution" Paragraph. Incorporate the following information and in the sequence listed below, as needed:

(1) cite page numbers of page replacements in the change transmittal;

(2) in the sequence in which they appear in the basic directive and/or enclosures;

(3) that "match" the page numbers to be replaced, including all page numbers that are not modified when these pages must be printed on the reverse side of the proposed page replacement;

(4) if the page numbers to be replaced do not match the page numbers to be inserted, cite all page numbers to be replaced and the new pages to be inserted; and

(5) of extended pages; e.g., 2a, 2b, 2c, in separate paragraphs.

g. "Summary of Change" Paragraph. If needed, include this paragraph to clarify the complexity of the change or to call attention to important changes.

h. "Filing Instructions" Paragraph. Include this paragraph to show where to file the change transmittal page(s).

43. Identifying Additional Pages of the Change Transmittal Page

a. Type the SSIC, change number, and date of the change (at top of page) like the basic directive to include the change number as shown below:

```
┌─────────────────────────────────────────────────────────────────────┐
│                                          MCO 5215.1J Ch 2             │
│                                          31 Aug 2003                  │
└─────────────────────────────────────────────────────────────────────┘
```

b. Page Replacements. Keep the original date and SSIC (at top) on all unchanged pages in the same position as the replaced pages.

44. Signing the Change Transmittal with a Revised Signature Page. If the basic directive was an MCO and the change is a modification of policy and procedures, the change must be signed at the same level as the original directive, or higher.

45. Maintaining Directives Files

a. Official Directives File. Each department or command originating directives will establish an official file. The official directive file will be maintained by the DCP, per reference (d). The file will include the original directive (signed copy) and all changes, revisions, supporting and other related background documents, to include approvals, and significant comments.

b. The official background file provides a history of the directive from its origin until cancelled. The cancelled document becomes the department's/command's document that originated the directive; the need to issue; the drafter's organization code; and the original date. The background material can be retrieved for official research and investigation matters.

c. <u>Disposition of Official Directive Files</u>. The official file will be disposed of per reference (d).

46. <u>Master Directive File</u>

a. The original directive issued by the CMC or command will be filed in the command's master directive file by the DCP.

b. <u>Filing</u>

(1) <u>Locator Sheets</u>. File in numerical sequence by SSIC in the master directive file, if applicable.

(2) <u>Cross-Reference Sheets</u>. File all cross-reference sheets in front of orders with the same SSIC.

(3) <u>Joint Publications</u>. File joint publications that are designated as MCOs in the master directive files.

47. <u>Checklists</u>

a. A checklist of current and cancelled directives may be issued. A numerical listing of all directives via web site is authorized.

b. A checklist may be issued on a quarterly, semi-annual, or annual basis.

c. If issued, include the following in your checklist:

(1) SSIC, consecutive number, and revision suffix letter.

(2) Original date of the basic directive. Do not show dates of changes.

(3) Number of changes issued to a directive.

(4) Security classification symbol (if any).

(5) Subject (may be abbreviated). Show an unclassified subject, abbreviation, or acronym for a classified directive.

(6) Sponsor's organizational code.

48. <u>Significant Pages Required in an Order</u>. Pages required are arranged in the order listed below:

a. Locator Sheet. The locator sheet is the first page after the cover letter in a directive, and is optional. Identify as page number "i". Refer to figure 1-3 for format.

b. Record of Changes

(1) The record of changes page provides a place to list new and revised editions. This is the page before the table of contents, and is optional. Identify as page number "ii". If a Locator Sheet is not needed, the Record of Changes must be identified as page number "i". Refer to figure 1-4 for format.

(2) The revised pages are printed and inserted in an Order, record the change number that transmitted the revised pages, in numerical sequence, and complete the remaining columns.

c. Table of Contents. Chapter numbers and titles in the table of contents must be in all capital letters. Show the chapter numbers and titles, appendix letters and titles, and page numbers. Include an index, if applicable. Identify the first page number of the table of contents as "iii". If a Locator Sheet or Record of Changes is not needed; the first page must be identified as page number "i". Figure 1-5 and pages iii thru v of this directive apply.

d. Reports Required

(1) Prepare a "Reports Required" page when there are five or more different reports in the Order. Refer to figure 1-6.

(2) When the "Reports Required" page is included, it must be the next page after the signature page. For example: If the signature page is page 4, the "Reports Required" page is page 5.

49. Directives Identification Block. Orders will show a running header (abbreviated identification) flushed with right margin and the date the directive was signed on the next line (day-month-year). If the directive is classified or must be printed, type the directives identification flushed with the upper right margin of odd numbered pages and upper left margin of even number pages. See paragraph 21.

50. Main Segments of Procedural Guidance (Enclosure to the Order). The main body of the enclosure is broken down into five distinct segments: chapter, figure, table, appendix, and index. Use only the segments that are needed.

a. Chapter(s)

(1) Chapters are the main segments in the enclosure.

(2) Use an Arabic numeral for number of the chapter; include the title heading on a separate line (single-line space if title is more than one line), and center all lines as shown printed in this Order.

(3) On the first page of text, style the title heading the same way it is styled on the Table of Contents page.

b. Figure

(1) When figures are used, cite them in the text in the sequence in which they are first mentioned.

(2) If there is no room to incorporate figures in the text, start the first figure on the page immediately following the end of the text of the segment in which first mentioned.

(3) At the bottom of the figure, type "Figure", chapter number, figure number followed by the title as shown below:

Figure 1-1.--First Figure.

Figure 1-1.--First Figure That Extends to More Pages--Continued

Figure 1-2.--Second Figure That has More Than One Line.

Figure 1-3.--Third Figure That has More Than One Line and Extends to More Pages--Continued

---

c. Table

(1) Show the title heading of a table at the top of the table in the same format style as for a figure, as shown above.

(2) When tables are included along with figures, start the first table on the page immediately following the end of the figures of the segment in which first mentioned.

(3) List tables at the end of the figure listing on the individual contents page in the same style as a figure listing.

(4) All other instructions that pertain to figures apply in the preparation of tables.

d. Appendix

(1) When appendixes are included, they shall appear at the end of the final chapter.

(2) Use all capital letters to identify an appendix; e.g., APPENDIX A, APPENDIX B, etc. Refer to figure 1-7.

e. Index

(1) When an index is included, it is the final segment of the enclosure and is inserted immediately following the final appendix.

(2) Arrange an index in alphabetical order by subject or key word. Show the paragraph, figure, or table number that contains the information. Refer to figure 1-8.

51. <u>Structuring Major Paragraph Numbers</u>. Follow instructions provided in reference (f) and chapter 1, paragraph 33.

52. <u>Numbering Pages</u>

a. Pages are numbered using Arabic numerals. Center and type the page number on all pages. Follow the method of numbering pages as shown in this Order. Start with Chapter and Number, Ex. 1-1, 2-1, or 3-1.

b. Prefix the page numbers of an appendix with the letter of the appendix; e.g., A-1. Prefix the page numbers of indexes as follows: I-1, I-2, or I-3.

53. <u>Preparing Change Transmittal Pages</u>. Follow guidance in chapter 1, paragraphs 40 through 44.

54. <u>Identifying and Replacing Chapters of an Order</u>. When a chapter is revised or <u>new</u> ones added, identify all pages with the change number at the top of all pages in the directives identification block.

Command Letterhead
Address

DIVO 1301.2A
(Office Code)
(Date Signed)

DIVISION ORDER 1301.2A

From: Commanding General
To: Distribution List

Subj: ASSUMPTION OF COMMAND

Ref: (a) U.S. Navy Reg. 1990, art. 0703 or appropriate
           reference
       (b) (Use appropriate reference)

1. Situation. To publish an assumption of command as required by
reference (a).

2. Cancellation. DIVO 1301.2. (Predecessor's order.)

3. Execution. I have assumed duties as Commanding General,
_____, this date as directed
by reference (b). All effective orders and directives issued by my
predecessors remain in effect.

                        PRINCIPAL'S NAME

DISTRIBUTION:

    Copy to: Seniors in chain-of-command (as directed by higher
              authority).
              Subordinate units.
          Senior commanders of other United States armed services
          and officials of other Federal agencies and foreign
          governments as appropriate (reference (a) above
          applies).

NOTE: 1. Use SSIC "1301" for an assumption of command order.
       2. Assign a new consecutive number to your order and cancel
           your predecessor's order.
       3. Revise your order, if needed, during your tour of duty.

       Figure 1-1.--Format of an Assumption of Command Order

DEPARTMENT OF THE NAVY
HEADQUARTERS UNITED STATES MARINE CORPS
3000 MARINE CORPS PENTAGON
WASHINGTON, DC 20350-3000

MCO 1000.1 Ch 1
ARDB
(Date Signed)

MARINE CORPS ORDER 1000.1 Ch 1

From: Commandant of the Marine Corps
To: Distribution List

Subj: FORMAT OF A CHANGE TRANSMITTAL

Encl: (1) New page inserts to MCO 1000.1

1. Situation. To transmit new page inserts to the basic order.

2. Additional Paragraphs. Refer to paragraph 42 chapter 1.

3. Execution

    a. Remove the letterhead page and page 2, and replace with corresponding pages in the enclosure.

    b. Remove Table of Contents and replace with corresponding Table of Contents contained in the enclosure.

    c. Insert new pages 2, 4a, 4b, and 4c in the basic order.

    d. Remove enclosures (1) and (2) and replace with corresponding enclosures contained in enclosure (1).

    e. Remove Appendices A through G and replace with corresponding Appendices contained in enclosure (1).

    f. The Reserve Applicability paragraph is not repeated in change transmittals.

                        I. M. COMMANDANT

DISTRIBUTION STATEMENT A: Approved for public release; distribution is unlimited.

            Figure 1-2.--Format of an MCO Change Transmittal

MCO 1000.1 Ch 1
(Date Signed)

DISTRIBUTION: PCN 10207570000

    Copy to: 8145001 (2)
              7000260 (1)

2

Figure 1-2.—-Format of a MCO Change Transmittal—Continued

MCO 5000.1
(Date Signed)

LOCATOR SHEET

Subj: _____

Location: _____
               (Indicate location(s) of copy(ies) of this
               Order.)

1. Type the SSIC and date at the upper right corner as shown here.

2. File this sheet like a directive in the master directives file.

3. Prepare a locator sheet for classified Orders. Do not show a classified subject; use an unclassified short title, if one, or type "SECRET" OR "CONFIDENTIAL."

4. The locator sheet is not used in place of "charge out" cards.

5. The locator sheet may be used to show your internal distribution, directives cancelled by the Order, or other related requirements.

i   Enclosure (1)

Figure 1-3.--Format of a Locator Sheet

RECORD OF CHANGES

Log completed change action as indicated.

Change Number	Date of Change	Date Entered	Signature of Person Incorporated Change

ii   Enclosure (1)

Figure 1-4.--Format of Record of Changes Page

MCO 5000.1
(Date Signed)

TABLE OF CONTENTS

iii   Enclosure (1)

Figure 1-5.--Format of a Table of Contents Page

MCO 5000.1
(Date Signed)

Reports Required

REPORT

REPORT TITLE	CONTROL SYMBOL	PARAGRAPH
I. Xxxxx Xxx Xxxxxx	MC-5215-01	2
II. Xxxxxx Xxxxxxx Xxx	MC-5215-02	3a
III. Xxx Xxxx Xxxxxxx	EXEMPT	4b(2)(a)
IV. Xx Xxxx Xxxxx	MC 5215-03	encl. (1)
V. Xxx Xxxx Xxxxx	MC-5215-04	encl. (2)

1. Use initial capital letters for major words in the report title.

2. Type all Roman numerals in capital letters and block as shown in this figure.

3. Cite the reports in the sequence in which they first appear in the Order.

4. Follow the format shown here when preparing a Reports Required page.

5

Figure 1-6.--Format of a Reports Required Page

MCO 5000.1
(Date Signed)

APPENDIX A

DECISION PACKAGE SETS (DPS'S)

A. General

1. Purpose. This appendix provides guidance concerning the processing of SECDEF decision package sets (DPS's) and the preparation of position papers and reclamas to support requested restoration of budget cuts.

2. Background. The OSD/OMB joint budget review normally begins in October and continues until its termination in December. The DPS's are the administrative process which reflects OSD/OMB budget decisions. There are five types of DPS's issued during the DPS cycle, each having a different purpose:

    a. Advance DPS's. Distributed for planning and research purposes. No formal action required.

    b. Action DPS's. These are numbered DPS's which constitute the tentative SECDEF decision. Subsequent to review by the appropriate staff agency, they are either accepted, reclamaed or made the subject of a position paper.

    c. Decision DPS's. These are DPS's which reflect SECDEF decisions on submitted reclamas. No action is required; however, the decision may be reclamaed during the Major Budget Issue (MBI) process. MBI's are discussed in detail elsewhere in this appendix.

    d. DPS Changes. These are changes to previously issued action or decision DPS's. Changes to action DPS's may be reclamaed.

    e. Wrap-Up DPS's. Normally issued at the end of the budget review to account for all changes to the budget. During the DPS cycle, hundreds of DPS's are issued by OSD. At the beginning of the cycle, a 72-hour deadline is established in which reclamas and position papers must be delivered to ASN (FM&C) from the time the DPS is received by DON.

A-1   Enclosure (1)

Figure 1-7.--Format of an Appendix

```
                                                    MCO 5000.1
                                                    (Date Signed)
                           INDEX

                             A

Acceptance of officer appointment:
     Enlisted to accept permanent officer appointment. .  page # can be found
     Enlisted to accept temporary officer appointment. . . .
     Reserve officer to accept permanent appointment . . . .
     Temporary officer appointment terminated to accept permanent
     Appointment . . . . . . . . . . . . . . . . . . . . . .
     Termination of temporary appointment to accept another
     Temporary appointment . . . . . . . . . . . . . . . . .
     To accept officer appointment from a "drop" status. . .
Accession of computer records into JUMPS/MMS . . . . . . . .
Accession of Transcription Form (ATP). . . . . . . . . . . .
Accumulated deployed time. . . . . . . . . . . . . . . . . .
Action statement – unit diary. . . . . . . . . . . . . . . .
Activation and deactivation of subunits. . . . . . . . . . .
Activation of a unit/command with a record of events entry .
Active naval service base date (permanent LDO's Only). . . .
Actual training completion date. . . . . . . . . . . . . . .
Administrative Control Unit (ACU). . . . . . . . . . . . . .
AFQT (Armed Forces Qualification Test) . . . . . . . . . . .
Alignment line . . . . . . . . . . . . . . . . . . . . . . .
Anniversary month (REPMIS) . . . . . . . . . . . . . . . . .
Appellate leave  . . . . . . . . . . . . . . . . . . . . . .
Applicant Qualification Test (AQT) . . . . . . . . . . . . .
Armed forces active duty base date . . . . . . . . . . . . .
Armed Forces Qualification Test (AFQT), Applicant Qualification Test (AQT)
and
```

```
                   I-1                          Enclosure (1)
```

Figure 1-8.--Format Guide for an Index

Chapter 2

Orders

1. Introduction. This chapter provides the instructions and format for preparing a "5-paragraph order" directive type designated as an order. Figure 2-1 depicts the format of a HQMC Marine Corps Order (MCO) and figure 2-2 depicts the format of a Field Command Order.

2. Letterhead Page

    a. Show the SSIC and the sponsor code in the upper right margin as "MCO 5215.1K" Add the date once the directive is signed.

    b. Start the designation line on the second line below the date in all capital letters; show as "MARINE CORPS ORDER 5215.1K."

    c. "From:" Line. Show principal official title; start on the second line below the designation line.

    d. "To:" Line. Insert "Distribution List;" start on the next line below the "From:" line.

    e. "Subj:" Line. Show in all capital letters; start on the second line below the "To:" line.

    f. "Ref:" Section. If any, start on the second line below the last line of the "Subj:" line.

    g. "Encl:" Section. If any, start on the second line below the last line of the "Ref:" line.

    h. "Distribution Statement" Block. Show at the bottom of the letterhead page. Refer to chapter 1 for the various distribution statements.

3. Mandatory Paragraphs

    a. "Situation" Paragraph. This paragraph describes the purpose, and must be the first paragraph of the directive.

    b. "Cancellation" Paragraph. This is always the second paragraph, if needed. Show the directives being canceled; show the SSIC of a bulletin and include the date of the "basic" bulletin. Only cancel directives you sponsor.

    c. "Mission" Paragraph. This paragraph describes the task to be accomplished; clear, concise statements of tasks. When cancellation of an MCO is required, a "Cancellation." paragraph will be paragraph "2", and the "Mission." paragraph will be paragraph "3". A cancellation paragraph is required when canceling other directives. When the "Cancellation" and "Mission" paragraphs are both used, the directive will have 6 paragraphs.

    d. "Execution" Paragraph. This paragraph contains clear and concise statements of the commander's intent to implement the directive to accomplish the mission. Amplifies paragraph 2, "Mission." The paragraph breakdowns into the following subparagraphs:

    (1) <u>Commander's Intent and Concept of Operations</u>

        (a) <u>Commander's Intent</u>. See figure 2-1

        (b) <u>Concept of Operations</u>. See figure 2-2

    (2) <u>Subordinate Element Missions</u>. This paragraph describes the main effort, supporting efforts, and Reserve.

    (3) <u>Coordinating Instructions</u>. This paragraph identifies and discusses instructions that are common to two or more elements, coordinating details.

4. <u>"Administration and Logistics" Paragraph</u>. This paragraph describes logistics, specific responsibilities, and support.

5. <u>"Command and Signal" Paragraph</u>. This paragraph breaks down into the following subparagraphs:

    a. <u>Command</u>. This paragraph provides the applicability statement; e.g., "This Order is applicable to the Marine Corps Total Force" or "This Order is applicable to the Marine Corps Reserve."

    b. <u>Signal</u>. This Order is effective the date signed.

6. <u>Signature Block</u>. The signature block appears as one of the following:

    a. When the CMC signs, show as follows:

    I. M. COMMANDANT

    b. When the ACMC signs, show as follows:

    I. M. ASSISTANTCOMMANDANT
    Assistant Commandant
    of the Marine Corps

    c. When a Deputy Commandant signs, show as follows:

    I. M. DEPUTYCOMMANDANTFORM&RA
    Deputy Commandant for
    Manpower and Reserve Affairs

    d. When an individual is acting in any one of the above capacity, show as follows:

    I. M. ACTINGCOMMANDANT
    Commandant of the Marine Corps
    Acting

I. M. ACTINGASSISTANTCOMMANDANT
Assistant Commandant of the
Marine Corps
Acting

I. M. ACTINGDEPUTYCOMMANDANTFORM&RA
Deputy Commandant for Manpower
and Reserve Affairs
Acting

    e. When issued by field commands, show as follows:

I. M. DIRECTOR   I. M. DEPUTY   I. M. EXECUTIVE
Chief of Staff   Deputy   Executive Officer

7. "DISTRIBUTION:" and "Copy to:" Sections

    a. Show the word "DISTRIBUTION:" at the left margin, second line after
signature block.

    b. Show the "Copy to:" on second line after "DISTRIBUTION:" indented
with colons aligned.

DEPARTMENT OF THE NAVY
HEADQUARTERS UNITED STATES MARINE CORPS
3000 MARINE CORPS PENTAGON
WASHINGTON, DC 20350-3000

MCO 5215.1J
ARDB
(Date Signed)

MARINE CORPS ORDER 5215.1J

From: Commandant of the Marine Corps
To: Distribution List

Subj: FIVE-PARAGRAPH ORDER FORMAT

Ref: (a) CMC Policy Memo 3-00 of 25 June 2000

1. Situation. Per the reference, policy-based directives that impact the commanders in the field shall be written as Marine Corps directives in a 5-paragraph order format. This figure provides the proper format.

2. Cancellation. MCO 5215.1H. (List cancelled directives, if any).

3. Mission. The mission statement provides the reason why the order was written. It answers the who, what, where, when, and why questions regarding the order.

4. Execution

    a. Commander's Intent and Concept of Operations

        (1) Commander's Intent

            (a) The commander's intent is the commander's personal expression of the purpose of the order.

            (b) It must be clear, concise, and easily understood.

DISTRIBUTION STATEMENT A: Approved for public release; distribution is unlimited.

Figure 2-1.--Five Paragraph Order Format

MCO 5215.1J
(Date Signed)

(c) It may also include how the commander envisions achieving a decision, as well as the end state or conditions that accomplish the purpose.

(2) <u>Concept of Operations</u>. The concept of operations is an overview of how the commander plans to accomplish the mission. It further answers the who, what, where, when and why questions.

b. <u>Subordinate Element Missions</u>

(1) Comply with the intent of the reference and the content of this Order.

(2) Directive sponsors are responsible for ensuring that their directives are in the correct format.

c. <u>Coordinating Instructions</u>. Submit all recommendations concerning this Order or Marine Corps directives in general to CMC (ARDB) via the appropriate chain of command.

5. <u>Administration and Logistics</u>

a. Distribution Statement "A" directives issued by CMC are published electronically and can be accessed online via the Marine Corps homepage at http://www.usmc.mil and MCPEL CD-ROM.

b. Access to an online medium will suffice for directives that can be obtained from the Internet, CD-ROM, or other sources.

6. <u>Command and Signal</u>

a. <u>Command</u>. This Order is applicable to the Marine Corps Total Force.

b. <u>Signal</u>. This Order is effective the date signed.

W. L. NYLAND
Assistant Commandant
of the Marine Corps

2

Figure 2-1.--Five Paragraph Order Format--Continued

MCO 5215.1J
(Date Signed)

DISTRIBUTION: PCN

   Copy to: 8145001 (2)
             7000260 (1)

3

Figure 2-1.--Five Paragraph Order Format--Continued

Unit Address

XXO SSIC.XX
Sponsor code
(Date Signed)

ACTIVITY CODE/NAME SSIC.XX (e.g., BATTALION ORDER SSIC.XX)

From: Commanding Officer or Officer In Charge
To: Distribution List

Subj: SAMPLE FIVE PARAGRAPH ORDER FORMAT

Ref: (a) (If applicable)

Encl: (1) (If applicable)

1. Situation. This paragraph describes the purpose and must be the
first paragraph of the directive.

2. Mission. Task to be accomplished. When cancellation of an order
is required, a "Cancellation" paragraph will be paragraph "2", and the
"Mission" paragraph will be paragraph "3". A cancellation paragraph is
required when canceling other directives and by higher authority
regulation. When the "Cancellation" and "Mission" paragraphs are both
used, the directive will have six paragraphs.

3. Execution

    a. Commander's Intent and Concept of Operations

        (1) Commander's Intent

        (2) Concept of Operations

    b. Subordinate Element Missions (main effort, supporting efforts,
and reserve efforts).

    c. Coordinating Instructions (identify and discuss instructions
that are common to two or more elements).

4. Administration and Logistics

DISTRIBUTION STATEMENT A: Approved for public release; distribution is
unlimited.

 Figure 2-2.--Five Paragraph Order Format for Field Commands

XXO SSIC.XX
(Date Signed)

5. Command and Signal

    a. Command. Reserve applicability.

    b. Signal. This (Order/Directive) is effective the date signed.

SIGNATURE BLOCK

DISTRIBUTION:

    Copy to:

2

Figure 2-2.—Five Paragraph Order Format for Field Commands--Continued

Chapter 3

Bulletins

1. Introduction. This chapter provides instructions and format for preparing a bulletin. Figures 3-1 through 3-3 provide samples.

2. Letterhead Page

   a. Cancellation Date. Type the cancellation date of a bulletin inside the upper right margin on the first page, on the second line above the normal position of the SSIC.

   b. If the cancellation date is for record purposes, with a contingent provision, type "Canc frp:" and abbreviate the month (a bulletin cancels on the last day), and use the four digit year; e.g., Canc frp: Sep 2007. Cancellation contingency is the condition that, when met, will satisfy the requirement(s) of a bulletin permitting cancellation. If cancellation of a bulletin is contingent on a specific action or event, the last paragraph of the bulletin must contain a brief description of the contingency. Once the action or event has been completed, the bulletin may be cancelled without waiting for the cancellation date. Refer to figure 3-1.

   c. If a bulletin cancels on a given date, with no contingency, show the cancellation date (as described above) like this: Canc: Sep 2007. Refer to figure 3-2.

3. SSIC and Sponsor Code. Show the SSIC and sponsor code in the upper right margin as "MCBul 1000." Add the date once the bulletin is signed.

4. Designation Line. Start the designation line on the second line below the date in all capital letters; show as "MARINE CORPS BULLETIN 1000."

5. "From:" Line. Show principal official title; start on the second line below the designation line.

6. "To:" Line. Insert "Distribution List"; start on the second line below the "From:" line.

7. "Subj:" Line. Show in all capital letters; start on the second line below the "To:" line.

8. "Ref:" Section. If any, start on the second line below the last line of the "Subj:" line.

9. "Encl:" Section. If any, start on the second line below the last line of the "Ref:" line.

10. "Distribution Statement" Block. Show at the bottom of the letterhead page. Refer to chapter 1 for the various distribution statements.

11. Major Paragraphs. The paragraphs below are the major paragraphs that appear in a bulletin. Other major paragraphs may be included, as applicable.

a. "Purpose" Paragraph. This paragraph is always first and gives the reason for the bulletin.

b. "Cancellation" Paragraph. This is always the second paragraph, if needed. Show the directives being canceled; show the SSIC of a bulletin and include the date of the "basic" bulletin. Only cancel directives you sponsor.

c. "Background" Paragraph. Include this paragraph, when needed, to provide any background information.

d. "Action" Paragraph. Include this paragraph to advise organizations/commands of specific action.

(1) Action required by a bulletin; e.g., submission of reports, use of forms, maintaining/disposing of records, or following a specific procedure, is canceled when the bulletin cancels, unless the requirement is incorporated into another suitable directive.

(2) If a bulletin with a given cancellation date has canceled and the material is still required, reissue the material in another suitable directive.

e. "Reserve Applicability" Paragraph. This paragraph provides the applicability statement; e.g., "This Directive is applicable to the Marine Corps Total Force" or "This Directive is applicable to the Marine Corps Reserve."

f. "Cancellation Contingency" Paragraph. Include as last paragraph, if the bulletin has a cancellation contingency. State the contingency, but do not repeat the cancellation date. Refer to figure 3-1.

12. Signature Block. The signature block appears as one of the following:

HQMC

I. M. ACTINGCOMMANDANT
Commandant of the Marine Corps
Acting

I. M. DEPUTYCOMMANDANTFORM&RA
Deputy Commandant for
Manpower and Reserve Affairs

I. M. ACTINGDEPUTYCOMMANDANTFORM&RA
Deputy Commandant for
Manpower and Reserve Affairs
Acting

Field Commands		
I. M. DIRECTOR Chief of Staff	I. M. DEPUTY Deputy	I. M. EXECUTIVE Executive Officer

13. "DISTRIBUTION:" and "Copy to:" Sections

   a. Show the word "DISTRIBUTION:" at the left margin, second line after signature block.

   b. Show the "Copy to:" on second line after "DISTRIBUTION:", indented with colons aligned.

14. Filing Instructions. If the bulletin cancels before it is incorporated into another directive, remove it and interfile it in the respective directive in the master file. Destroy the bulletin when it is incorporated in another directive.

15. Bulletins Issued in Message Format. The following provides instructions and format for preparing bulletins in message format. Figure 3-3 provides a sample.

   a. "FM" Line (In messages, the "from" line is shown as "FM")

      (1) In the "FM" line immediately following the principal's address, show a double slant mark (//) followed by the sponsor's organizational code.

      (2) Additional codes are separated by a single slant mark (/) and closed with the double slant mark.

   b. Classification: "UNCLASSIFIED," "CONFIDENTIAL," or "SECRET."

   c. "SUBJ" Line

      (1) Type the SSIC of the message on the same line with the "SUBJ/MCBUL 5000." and end with a period.

      (2) Allow two spaces after the period and type the subject. If the subject is more than one line, return to the original margin as follows:

UNCLASS//

SUBJ/MCBUL 5000. XXX XXXXXXXX XXXX XXXXXXX XXXX

XXXX XXXXXXXXXX XXXXX

---

   d. Cancellation. When a bulletin cancels another directive, show the bulletin being canceled in the second paragraph as follows:

Enclosure (1)

2.   MCO 1000.XX or MCBUL 5000 of 21 SEP 2002 IS CANCELED.

e.   Reports Required. When a report is required, type the "Report Required:" section at the left margin before the first paragraph and block the report subject if more than one line:

REPORT REQUIRED: SUBJECT OF THE REPORT (REPORT CONTROL
                   SYMBOL MC-5215-OT), PAR 4

f.   Releasing Authority. Bulletins are signed only by those officials designated. (See Chapter 1, Paragraph 7)

g.   Cancellation Date. A bulletin is automatically canceled in 12 months except when the text provides for an earlier cancellation.

h.   Clearance of Bulletins Issued by Message. Bulletins shall be staffed and cleared as per guidance provided in chapter 1.

i.   Background Material. After the transmission, a copy of the "signed" message, along with the originals of the background material and staff clearances shall be forwarded to the CMC (ARDB). Request a verbatim electronic file be provided to CMC (ARDE) with a signed copy for inclusion on the www.usmc.mil website and MCPEL CD-ROM.

DEPARTMENT OF THE NAVY
HEADQUARTERS UNITED STATES MARINE CORPS
3000 MARINE CORPS PENTAGON
WASHINGTON, DC 20350-3000

or

Unit Address

Canc frp: Oct 2004

MCBul or I MEFBul 1000
ARDB or G-1
(Date Signed)

MARINE CORPS BULLETIN 1000 or
I MEF BULLETIN 1000

From: Commandant of the Marine Corps or Commanding General
To: Distribution List

Subj: FORMAT OF A BULLETIN WITH A CANCELLATION
        CONTINGENCY

Ref: (a) MCO 5200.1
        (b) DoD Directive 5025.1, "DoD Directives System,"
            July 27, 2000

Encl: (1) Subject of First Enclosure
        (2) (SC) Show Exact Title of Enclosure Under Separate Cover

Reports Required: I.   Review of Publications (Report Control
                        Symbol MC-5600-OT), par. 2
                   II. Special Directives (Report Control Symbol
                        EXEMPT), par 3

1. Purpose. To show the format of a bulletin with a cancellation
contingency, per the references.

2. Cancellation. Identify directives being canceled, if any.

3. Background. Bulletins have the same force and effect as Orders, transmit
information, require action, request one-time reports, and are for a short
term.

DISTRIBUTION STATEMENT A: Approved for public release; distribution is
unlimited.

            Figure 3-1.--Format of a Letter-Type Bulletin with a Cancellation
                        Contingency

MCBul or I MEFBul 1000
(Date Signed)

4. Action. Show the cancellation date inside the upper right margin on the first page, on the second line above the SSIC. If the cancellation date is for record purposes, with a contingency provision, abbreviate the month (cancels last day), and use the four digit year; e.g., "Canc frp: Oct 2007." Include as the last paragraph headed "Cancellation Contingency" and state the contingency but do not repeat the cancellation date.

5. Reserve Applicability. This Bulletin is applicable to the Marine Corps Total Force.

6. Cancellation Contingency. This Bulletin is canceled when incorporated in reference (a).

SIGNATURE BLOCK

DISTRIBUTION: PCN 10207570000

   Copy to: 8145001 (2)
             7000260 (1)

2

Figure 3-1.--Format of a Letter-Type Bulletin with a Cancellation
Contingency--Continued

DEPARTMENT OF THE NAVY
HEADQUARTERS UNITED STATES MARINE CORPS
3000 MARINE CORPS PENTAGON
WASHINGTON, DC 20350-3000

or

Unit Address

Canc: Oct 2004

MCBul or I MEF 1000
ARDB or G-1
(Date Signed)

MARINE CORPS BULLETIN 1000 or
I MEF BULLETIN 1000

From: Commandant of the Marine Corps or Commanding General
To: Distribution List

Subj: FORMAT OF A LETTER-TYPE BULLETIN WITH A GIVEN
       CANCELLATION DATE

Ref: (a) MCO 5200.1
       (b) DoD Directive 5025.1, "DoD Directives System,"
           July 27, 2000

Encl: (1) Subject of First Enclosure
       (2) (SC) Show Exact Title of Enclosure Under Separate Cover

Reports Required: I. Review of Publications (Report Control
                       Symbol MC-5600-OT), par. 2
                  II. Special Directives (Report Control Symbol
                       EXEMPT), par 3

1. Purpose. To show the format of a letter-type bulletin with a given
cancellation date, per the references.

2. Cancellation. Identify directives being canceled, if any.

3. Background. Letter-type bulletins have the same force and effect as
directives, transmit information, require action, request one-time reports,
and are for a short term.

DISTRIBUTION STATEMENT A: Approved for public release; distribution is
unlimited.

       Figure 3-2.—-Format of a Letter-Type Bulletin with a Given
                   Cancellation Date

MCBul or I MEFBul 1000
(Date Signed)

4. <u>Action</u>. Show the given cancellation date inside the upper right margin on the first page, on the second line above the SSIC. If the cancellation date is for record purposes, with a contingency provision, abbreviate the month (cancels last day), and use the four digit year; e.g., "Canc frp: Oct 2004." A self-cancellation paragraph is not required.

5. <u>Reserve Applicability</u>. This Bulletin is applicable to the Marine Corps Total Force.

SIGNATURE BLOCK

DISTRIBUTION: PCN 10207570000

    Copy to: 8145001 (2)
               7000260 (1)

2

Figure 3-2.--Format of a Letter-Type Bulletin with a Given
Cancellation Date--Continued

FM CMC WASHINGTON DC(UC)
TO AL MARADMIN(UC)
UNCLASSIFIED//
MARADMIN 465/06
MSGID/GENADMIN/CMC WASHINGTON DC MRA MM//
SUBJ/MCBUL 1400. OCTOBER 2006 REGULAR CORPORAL AND SERGEANT
/PROMOTION AUTHORITY//
REF/A/MSGID:DOC/MMPR-2/11MAY2006//
AMPN/REF A IS MCO P1400.32D, ENLISTED PROMOTION MANUAL//
POC/J.A. MCLAUGHLIN/MAJ/MMPR-2/-/TEL:DSN 278-9718
/EMAIL:JAMES.MCLAUGHLIN@USMC.MIL//
GENTEXT/REMARKS/1. USE THE MARINE CORPS TOTAL FORCE SYSTEM (MCTFS)
TO VIEW THE ACTIVE DUTY PROMOTION PARAMETERS FOR THE CURRENT
PROMOTION QUARTER AND THE ACTIVE DUTY CUTTING SCORES FOR THE CURRENT
PROMOTION MONTH. THIS MAY BE DONE BY TYPING "CCOS" FROM THE MCTFS
MAIN MENU AND THEN SELECTING THE DESIRED OPTION. CUTTING SCORES
SHOULD BE PRINTED FROM THE "CCOS" SCREEN AND ATTACHED WITH THIS
MARADMIN TO BE USED FOR FUTURE REFERENCE. NOTE THAT ANY MOS LISTED
ON THE "CCOS" SCREEN AS "9999" IS CLOSED FOR PROMOTION. CUTTING
SCORES ALSO WILL BE AVAILABLE ON THE ENLISTED PROMOTION SECTION WEB
PAGE.
2. TO ELIMINATE ERRONEOUS PROMOTIONS AND DELAYS IN PROMOTING
DESERVING MARINES, COMMANDERS WILL ENSURE THE FOLLOWING CRITERIA
ARE MET:
   A. RECEIPT OF THIS MARADMIN AS THE OFFICIAL PROMOTION AUTHORITY.
   B. RECEIPT OF 1 OCTOBER 06 SELECT GRADE GENERATED ON THE UNIT
DIARY FEEDBACK REPORT.
3. THE REF SETS FORTH GUIDANCE AND INSTRUCTIONS FOR EFFECTING THE
MONTHLY PROMOTION OF LCPL'S AND CPL'S OF THE REGULAR MARINE CORPS
WHO MEET THE FOLLOWING CRITERIA:
   A. SEL CPL ED: 20061001
   B. SEL SGT ED: 20061001
   C. DATE OF RANK: 20061001
   D. EFFECTIVE DATE: 20061001
4. FOR MARINE ENLISTED PROMOTION MATTERS CALL COMM (703) 784-9717
OR DSN 278-9717. E-MAIL INQUIRIES MAY BE SUBMITTED VIA THE
PROMOTION BRANCH'S INTERNET WEB PAGE AT WWW.USMC.MIL. SELECT
"CAREER", "MARINES", "PROMOTIONS", "ENLISTED", "CONTACTS".
5. THIS BULLETIN IS NOT APPLICABLE TO THE MARINE CORPS RESERVE.
6. THIS BULLETIN IS CANCELED 30 SEPTEMBER 2007.//

Figure 3-3.--Sample of a Bulletin Issued by Message

Chapter 4

Joint Directives

1. <u>Introduction</u>. This chapter provides supplemental information for preparing joint directives. Detailed instructions and format for preparing joint directives sponsored by the Marine Corps are contained in chapter 2. The Navy DCP controls the format of Navy-sponsored joint directives coordinated with HQMC. The following provides procedures for coordinating proposed directives between HQMC and Navy agencies.

    a. A joint directive is issued when uniformity, identical language, form, or timing is needed. The principal component that has the overall degree of responsibility for a particular effort is the primary principal and should act as the coordinator, as mutually agreed upon, to obtain clearances on a joint directive; grade or seniority of a principal is not the deciding factor.

    b. Joint directives issued at the field command will follow the procedures in this section.

    c. <u>Definitions</u>

        (1) <u>Joint Directive</u>. A directive issued in a single version by two or more independent principal components when a requirement for uniformity necessitates identical language, form, or timing.

        (2) <u>Coordinator</u>. The staff official of the primary principal who prepares and obtains clearances from other independent principal's agencies.

        (3) <u>Principal</u>. An independent issuing authority; e.g., Army, Navy, Air Force, and Marine Corps.

        (4) <u>Primary Principal</u>. The principal who has the overall degree of responsibility in a joint effort or as mutually agreed upon by all other participating independent principals.

        (5) <u>Common Superior</u>. The principal officer who has responsibility in decision-making for subordinate or independent components (may be dual-hatted); e.g., Secretary of the Navy.

        (6) <u>Principal Subordinates</u>. Principal officials who share the same common superior, but is authorized to promulgate directives in a single version under their titles and in their own systems; e.g., CMC, CNO, etc.

2. <u>SSIC and Signature Requirements</u>. It must be noted that only the SSIC of the primary principal is shown on a directive.

    a. <u>Intra-Navy Department Directives Coordinated at HQMC Level</u>

        (1) An intra-Navy directive coordinated with HQMC by a Navy Department principal is not assigned a Marine Corps SSIC. When needed, include a statement in the directive regarding HQMC level concurrence, and clarify the kind of action to be taken by subordinate units. The directive

will show only the SSIC and signature of the Navy Department principal.

(2) When cognizance of an intra-Navy directive subject matter is divided between the Navy principal and HQMC principal subordinate oversight authority or overlaps, the directive is then jointly signed over the title of each principal.

   b. Joint Directives Issued at the Field Command Level

(1) The primary principal must give preference to the promulgation of a directive by the next higher common superior. This is particularly relevant when additional duty or "dual-hatted" staffing exists.

(2) A directive that requires agreement between or among independent principal subordinates must be fully coordinated with all other participating principals for concurrence in a single version in the primary principal's system. The directive will carry only the SSIC and signature of the primary principal.

(3) When the subject matter is divided between principal subordinates or overlaps, the directive is then jointly signed over the title of each principal. The directive will carry only the SSIC of the primary principal.

   c. Directives that require agreement between the Reserve unit and the Inspector-Instructor staff will be coordinated and cleared by all participants and issued in the directives system of the commanding officer of the Reserve unit, who is the "principal" official. The Inspector-Instructor staff is an administrative body of the command; therefore, directives will be coordinated between these two elements to incorporate an approval/concurrence statement, clarify the extent or kind of action to be taken, and will carry the SSIC and signature of the principal official or the signer who has been formally appointed or delegated to replace temporarily the principal official. Inspector-Instructor staffs are authorized to promulgate directives to offices under their immediate authority and in their own system.

3. Applicability of Joint Directives. A joint directive is applicable to all addressees by Distribution List and Publications Control Number (PCN) in the same manner as a regular directive.

4. Canceling Joint Directives. The primary principal must obtain concurrence from all participating principals before a joint directive is cancelled. Justification must be provided to the primary principal stating the reason a joint directive is still needed by the other participants. The justification should include whether pertinent portions will be released in the respective principal's directives system or is only needed for a specific length of time.

5. Information Required for Joint Directives. The primary principal will obtain the following, in writing, from all participating principals, as applicable:

   a. Each principal's office code must be shown in the "Reply refer to:" position on the directive.

b. The title of the signer that makes up the signature block.

c. The distribution code(s) or list(s) of the participating principals when a joint directive is to be distributed to their subordinate units, to include the style and manner to be shown on the printed copies.

d. The method by which each participating principal's copies are to be procured and distributed, to include sharing the cost of printing by each principal, as applicable.

6. Checklist of Effective Directives. Joint directives will be identified and listed in the checklist of the primary principal, but may also be listed in the checklists of the other participating principals.

7. Preliminary Coordination

a. Preliminary work is normally done by a joint working group which resolves problems and details to mutual satisfaction and should determine at that time, if not previously decided, the primary principal and coordinator.

b. The preliminary draft is prepared by the coordinator of the primary principal for review by the working group level.

c. Differences or necessary changes concerning the preliminary draft are resolved before final coordination for signature and distribution instructions are obtained from all participants.

8. Final Coordination. The primary principal's coordinator will affect the following:

a. Prepare the directive in final form.

b. Obtain the signature of the cognizant principal subordinate, if it is not signed by a higher common superior.

c. Prepare and attach a brief to the directive for the signer's review to include:

(1) Background information.

(2) Reason for directive and scope.

(3) Summary of reciprocal action taken by other participants.

9. Signature Authority. Joint directives shall be approved and signed by the Commandant of the Marine Corps (CMC); the Assistant Commandant of the Marine Corps (ACMC); the Director, Marine Corps Staff; the Deputy Commandant for Manpower and Reserve Affairs; the Deputy Commandant for Installations and Logistics; the Deputy Commandant for Plans, Policies, and Operations; the Deputy Commandant for Aviation; the Deputy Commandant for Programs and Resources; or the Deputy Commandant for Combat Development and Integration. The Deputy Commandants shall sign, by title, policy for their departmental areas of responsibility. Field Command directives shall be approved and signed as delegated by the senior principal official.

10. Format of a Directive Signed by Two or More Principals. Follow the format of a joint letter-type order to include the following:

a. Show each principal's letterhead nomenclature on the letterhead page.

b. Show only the SSIC of the primary principal.

c. Include the organizational code symbol of each participating principal in the "In reply refer to:" position to identify the cognizant office of participating principals.

d. Include the titles of all principals in the "From:" line.

e. Show the primary principal's signature block ending at the right margin, the secondary principal's signature block even with the left margin, and the tertiary principal's signature blocked/centered.

f. Include the distribution code(s)/list(s)/IACs of all principals in the "DISTRIBUTION:" section.

g. Coordinate and prepare changes and revisions by following the same procedures that applied for the basic directive or the previous edition.

h. If additional guidance is needed, contact CMC (ARDB).

www.ingramcontent.com/pod-product-compliance
Lightning Source LLC
Chambersburg PA
CBHW080535290526
45790CB00006B/2413